MIND YOUR MOMENTS SERIES • BOOK ONE

Trees don't Rush

ANGELA BELL JULIEN

Trees Don't Rush

Copyright © 2017 Angela Bell Julien. All rights reserved. No part of this book may be reproduced or retransmitted in any form or by any means without the written permission of the publisher.

Published by Wheatmark®
2030 East Speedway Boulevard, Suite 106
Tucson, Arizona 85719 USA
www.wheatmark.com

ISBN: 978-1-62787-443-4
ISBN: 978-1-62787-444-1 (ebook)
LCCN: 2016949285

Also by Angela Bell Julien:
Blooms and the Bard: Painted Sonnets

To Paul Julien,
Who has supported every moment of this endeavor
and is my greatest fan.

Thank you to Jacob Chinn, *Jacob Chinn Photography*,
for photographing my paintings.

Nature's Moments Nurture the Spirit

Time is a valuable commodity. People always tell me that "time" is what keeps them from doing what they dream of doing, what they need to do, what they should do. They believe that time is not available to them. The truth? Time is everywhere. Time is ours to make, to destroy, to keep, to harbor. In fact, nature can teach us many lessons about time. Nature doesn't hurry; nature takes the time necessary to create beauty, to sculpt the greatest canyons and to bloom the tiniest and most fragile blossom—and the world waits.

My mother used to quote Lewis Carroll's White Rabbit to me, "the hurrier you go; the behinder you get." I so wish I had listened. I am afraid the first words my children knew were "hurry up." I wonder, what did we gain in life with all that hurry? I can't determine anything. Now, I heed my mother's words. Hurry just makes me make mistakes, feel over wrought and lose the light in life. I am learning to "mind my moments."

Trees Don't Rush is my new version of my mother's old adage. I believe the mindfulness movement is born of what has become a constantly hasty approach to life. In a conversation with a young man just graduating from high school, I listened to his dream of entering the world of music. He is a gifted musician and wants nothing more than to let his talent waft over the world. However, many people tell him that he doesn't have time. He needs to pick a serious endeavor and not get behind his peers in the race for what they call success. In our conversation, I talked to him about time, and that life is long. He has time to make his music and, if he chooses, seek other endeavors later.

I overheard a young woman tell a person urging her to use her skills to "get ahead" and live a more affluent lifestyle. She calmly replied that she loved her life, her walks in the park and her quiet, modest neighborhood. She was joyful; her dream is fulfilled in minding her moments.

Don't misunderstand, my life is busy; I still hasten too much. Appreciating the present takes great thoughtfulness.

Trees Don't Rush is my gift to all my fellow moment missers. The poems are meant to be read slowly, maybe one today and two tomorrow. The journal pages are for you to sit, be mindful and then record your reflections. May they lead you to finding great joy.

Nature's moments bring back the light. Illuminate your thoughts as you read and write.

Contents

Trees Don't Rush 1

Roots 5

All Dirt Roads Lead to Heaven 15

Life Is Long .21

Vanilla Trees .31

Tree of Many Colors 35

Mother Sun .39

Monsoon Moments 43

Love Above the Trees 49

Spirit Gift 55

When Words Falter 59

Wind 63

Evening Flower 67

A Moment's Perspective 73

Growing in the Moment 77

Tree of Hope 81

Blurred Moments 85

Playful Moments 89

Into the Hand I Hold 95

Trees Don't Rush

Trees don't rush
    To be strong

Trees know the moment
    And grow into it

Not hurry past it and
    Miss the meaning.

Trees don't rush

We should lie
    In their shade

Be still

And Learn.

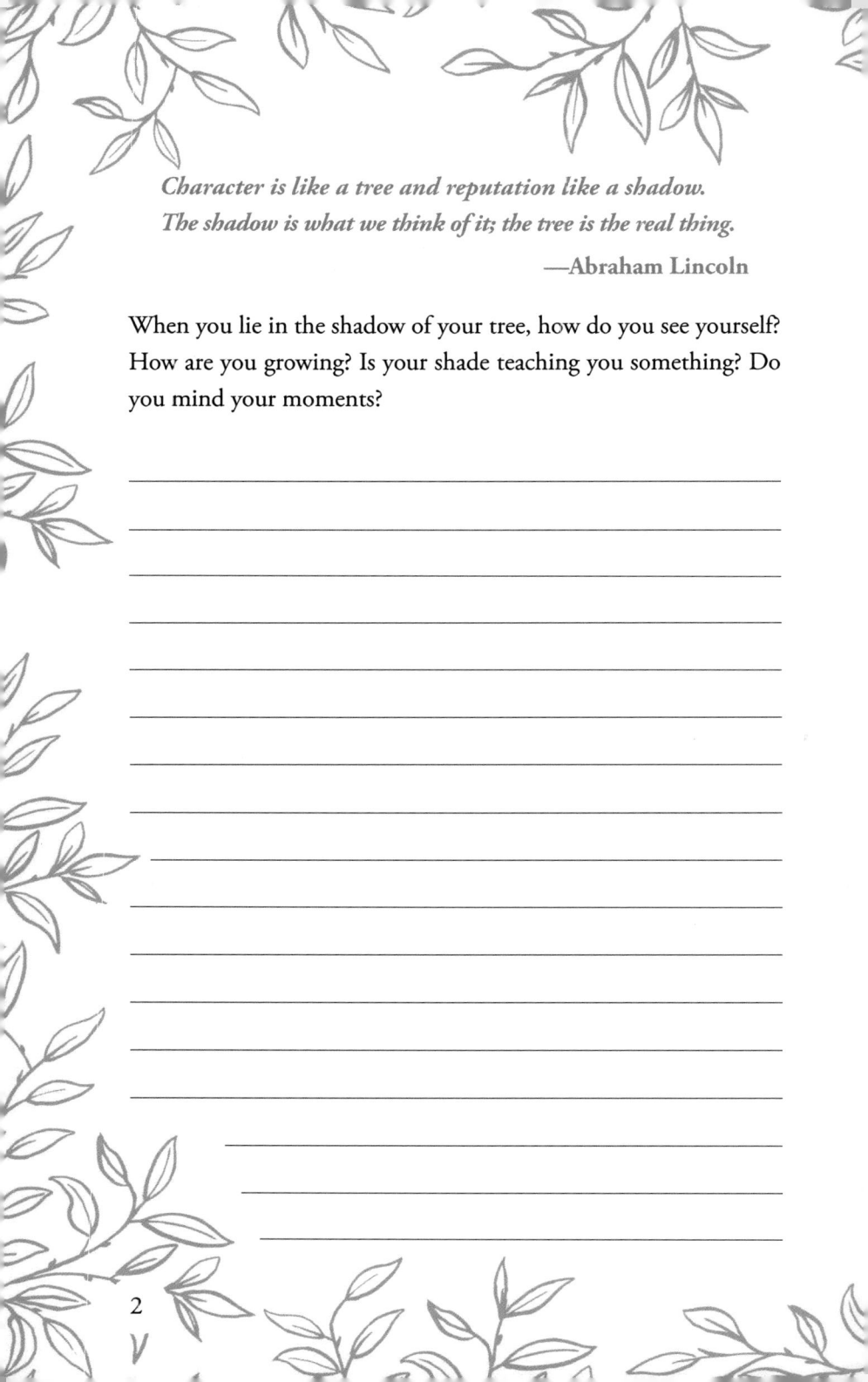

Character is like a tree and reputation like a shadow.
The shadow is what we think of it; the tree is the real thing.

—Abraham Lincoln

When you lie in the shadow of your tree, how do you see yourself? How are you growing? Is your shade teaching you something? Do you mind your moments?

Roots

Roots drive
into the earth

Slowly

Etching paths,
Patiently seeking

Nourishment

Veined bark
Unfolding

Limb by limb

Weaving a wooden
tapestry

Lifting

A great loom
Of life

Skyward

Shy buds
Bearing seeds

Infants,

Peer out beyond
the skirt of branches

Yawning

Building a canopy,
Earth's green

Parasol

Sifting sunlight
Drinking rain

Flowering

Giving voice
to peace

Before an autumnal
chill sparks and

Bursts

Fierce and fiery flashes
Of colors golden, red

And orange

That fade
before they

Loosen

And waft
in the wind

Dancing

To the earth
Intermingling there

A colorful crochet

Blanketing the browning
lawn

Leaving strong arms
Bearing the beauty of the cold

Silently

Enrapt in white and
Serving as a

Beacon

Of hope for
Future life

While

Roots drive
into the earth

Slowly
Etching paths,
Patiently seeking

Nourishment.

Veined bark
Unfolding

Limb by limb

Seasons repeat, renewing. Taking the time to try again, improve upon what has been helps me to be mindful of small improvements I can make in my own life.

Where are your roots taking you?

All Dirt Roads Lead to Heaven

Pavement ends
Rugged bumps begin
My eyes fall shut
But I can see

Dirt road
Heavy load

Distant peak
Bright blue eyes
In the rear view mirror
Smiling down on me

Pavement ends
Rugged bumps begin
I hide my head
In pillowed fear
But I can hear

Dirt road
Heavy load

Tires scrape
In rock and sand

Loud thump
"just a bump"
his chuckle
and his grin

Pavement ends
Rugged road begins
I lock my door
clutch the grip
But I can feel

Dirt road
Heavy load

An arm reaches out
And holds me safe
But lets me bounce
Just enough
To make the story good

Sitting by my
Father's side

All dirt roads
Lead to heaven

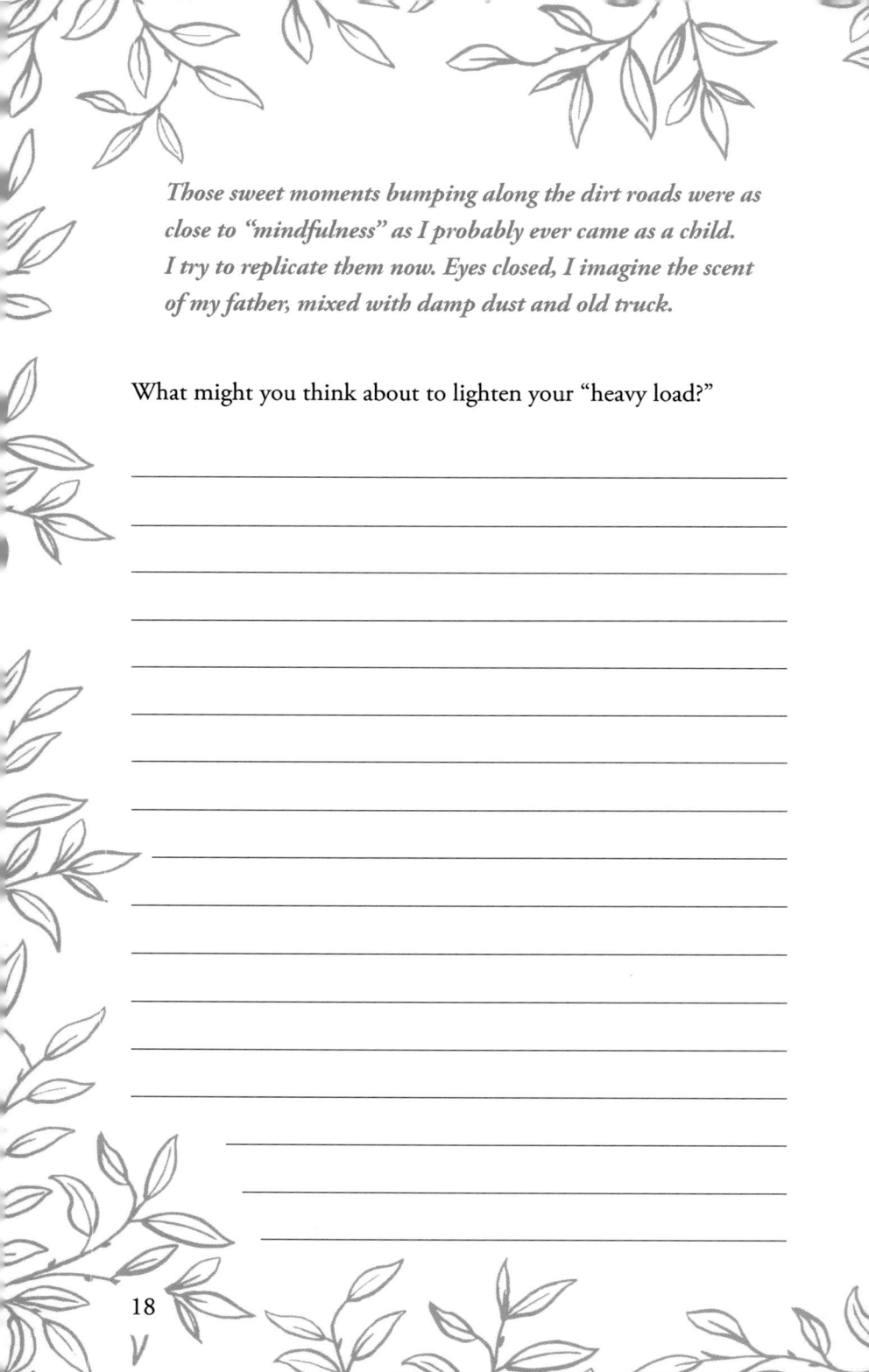

Those sweet moments bumping along the dirt roads were as close to "mindfulness" as I probably ever came as a child. I try to replicate them now. Eyes closed, I imagine the scent of my father, mixed with damp dust and old truck.

What might you think about to lighten your "heavy load?"

_____
_____
_____
_____
_____
_____
_____
_____
_____
_____
_____
_____
_____
_____
_____
_____
_____
_____

Life Is Long

The greatest myth
imposed upon the human race
is that

Life is short.

The Myth incites the rush
That cuts laughter short

And curls the mind
into tight knots
of thought

served up as sound bites

without plot,

without reason,

without color

Life is long

An epic tale
The knotted brain

untangles slowly,

Mindful of detail
With time to write
multiple iterations
of the future

Allowing youth to dream

Unimpeded by limitations of

Timed sprints
Encouraging meditated,

thoughtful movement

Not assertions wrought
With angst of

Life is short

Life is long

Hurry is a curse
Life comes by
And lingers

Lingers longer when

Savored

Sipped.

"Walk in beauty"
the ancients said.

Not run in haste
To grab the best

Be the first

Finish fast

"Walk in beauty"
lost in deep reflection

Mindful of the Moment

Extending life
Past sharp edges
into disentangled streams

Flowing breath
To breath

Life is long

Sigh,

Sit back

And row.

Thinking about "life is long" encourages me to think about the "new" parts of life—start writing a new book, painting more, kayaking.

Life is long?
How does that change the way you might approach life?

"Walk in beauty" is a concept from a traditional Navajo/Diné prayer. When I first heard it, I thought walking in beauty meant finding a pretty place for a walk. Now, I realize, it is the way I approach the people and the places I meet. The beauty is within me and when I "walk in beauty" I find the grace in life.

Lord Byron's poem "She Walks In Beauty" follows the same path.

How will you "walk in beauty?"
What will it reveal?

_____
_____
_____
_____
_____
_____
_____
_____
_____
_____
_____
_____
_____
_____
_____
_____

I want to linger and extend my life past the sharp edges of actions taken in short spurts. As a child, I moved quickly from task to task. Even on vacation, I rush from one activity to the next. I do not stop to ask questions, to ponder. Sometimes being "finished" is more important than being thoughtful. I believe I am "multi-tasking" when actually I am just ignoring the soft side of life. That translates into missing moments of wonder and awe. I need to linger.

Where are your sharp edges?

_____
_____
_____
_____
_____
_____
_____
_____
_____
_____
_____
_____
_____
_____

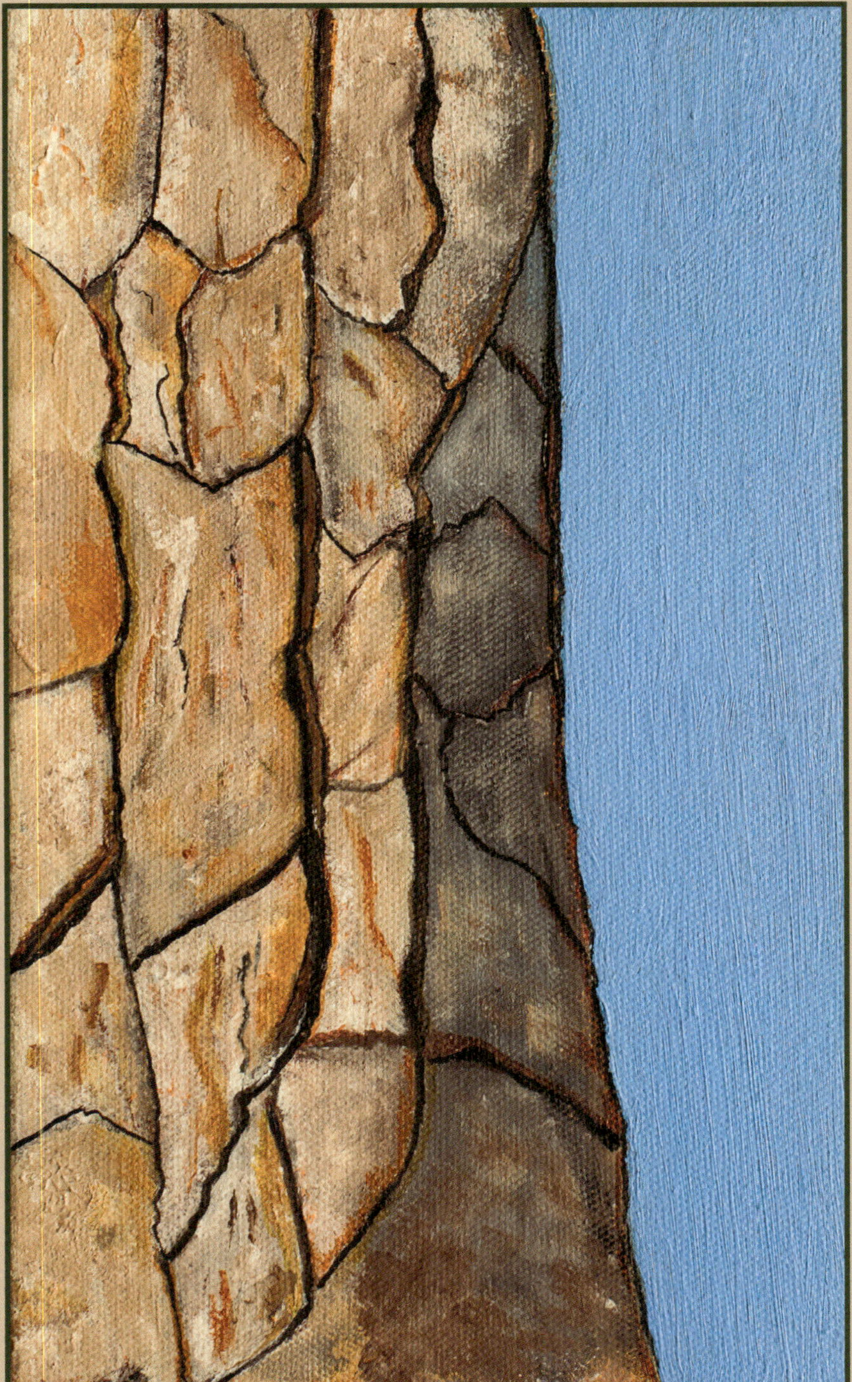

Vanilla Trees

The latte skin, marbled cream and caramel
Sits juxtaposed against a sky of pure
Unblemished blue. The rugged texture lures
A hand—to feel the tale the tree can tell.

A wanderer will trod the wooded peaks
Allowed to touch the Braille of aged past
And read the milky moments that will outlast
The answers human interlopers seek.

Some souls are satisfied to touch the bark
Of giants looming heavenward and think
The plot lies only there. They do not drink
Of what lives within the skin. The veins of dark

And syruped scent. The few who deeply breathe
Discover secrets hidden in Vanilla Trees.

I lived among the Ponderosa Pines for many years before I knew that if you press your nose closely to the bark of an older tree, you will smell the sweet aroma of vanilla. Some people say it is like smelling cookies baking. I wonder how many other sweet smells I have missed by rushing through my moments?

What details might you have been missing.
What do you want to discover?

_____
_____
_____
_____
_____
_____
_____
_____
_____
_____
_____
_____
_____

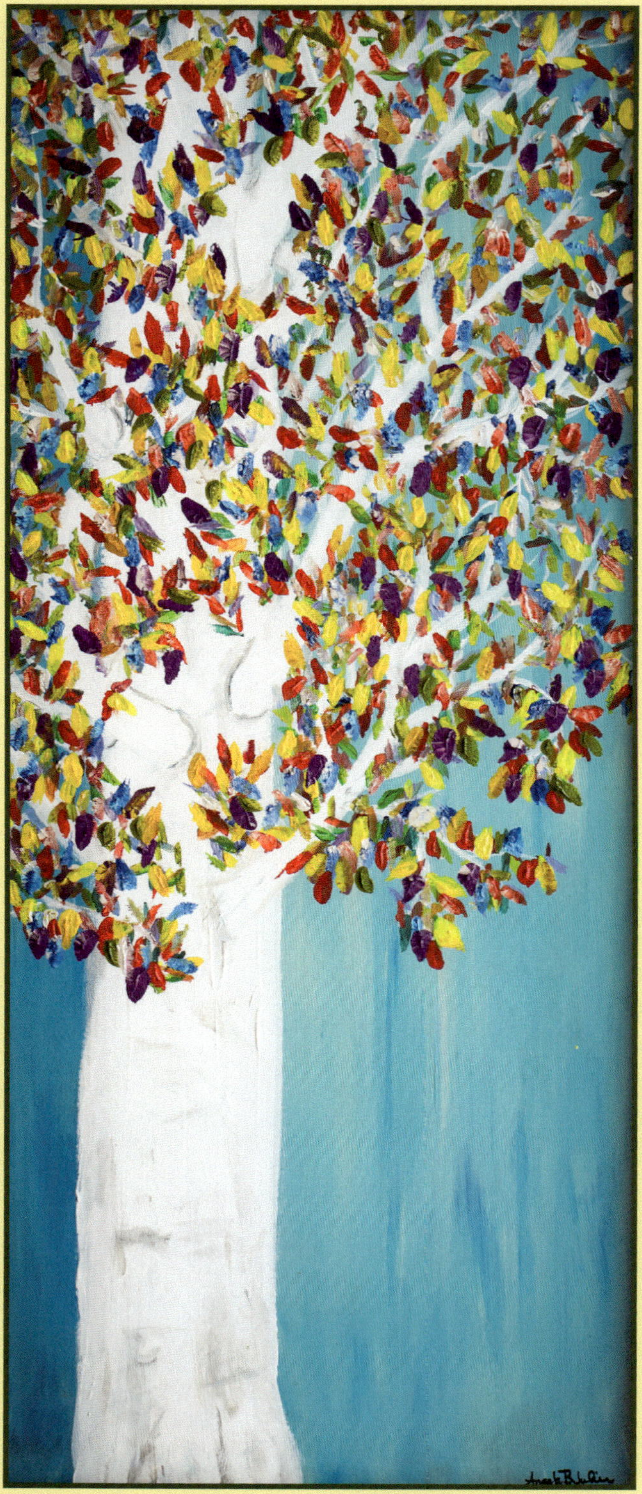

Tree of Many Colors

A tree

Of many colors

Exists inside my mind

Sharing it takes courage

For some would find

it foolish

And others look

beyond to teach me

The truth, that trees

Only green will be

—Or red

and yellow

Only in the fall

But a tree

Of colors all

Has lived behind

My eyes

A lifetime, maybe more.

Are we who see the hues

thinking clearly, unrestrained

Or drenched in Mitty's muse?

"Mitty" is an allusion to the title character in James Thurber's short story, "The Secret Life of Walter Mitty." Many people are more aware of the character from the newer movie based on the short story. As a child I was a great "pretender." I loved to imagine what "might be."

Colors have always sparked my imagination.
Sometimes I forget to look at all the possibilities now.
What is your favorite daydream?

_____
_____
_____
_____
_____
_____
_____
_____
_____
_____
_____
_____
_____

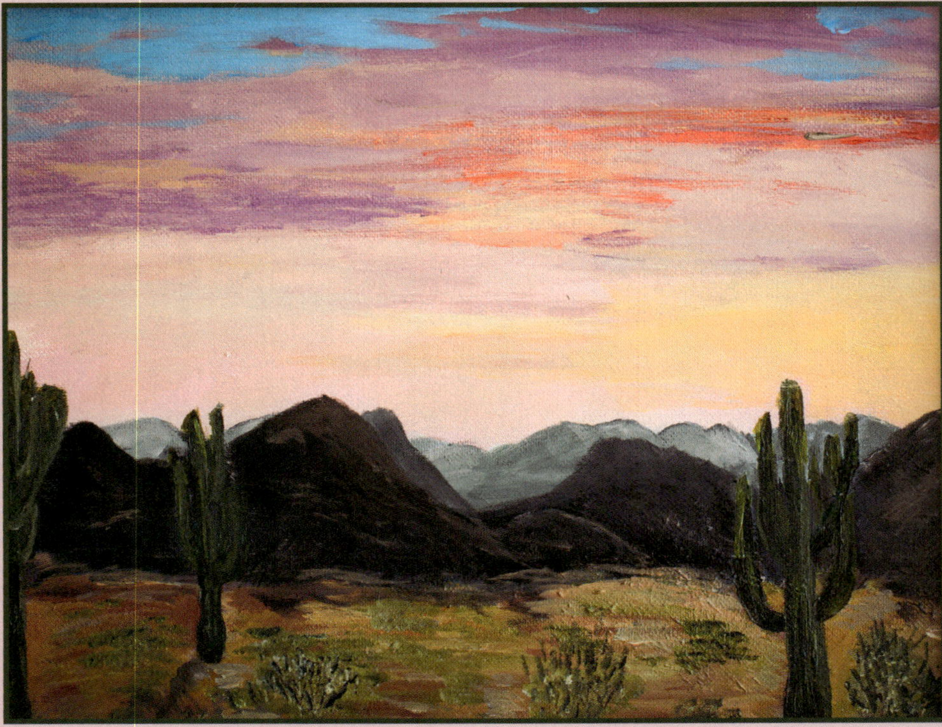

Mother Sun

Mother sun
Feigns softness,
Peeks past
Distant blue-gray
hills.

Brushes scenes
Kaleidoscoped in color

To lure
The lazy
Out of shadows

Capturing energy,
Dancing
Into life's

Stained glass
Moments,

Tempered heat
Melts morning
And sizzles

Into day.

A time to weep, and a time to laugh; a time to mourn, and a time to dance. —Ecclesiastes 3:4

Do I dance into "life's stained glass moments?" Not enough, but I am learning. I can see the colors shine through the glass—now to learn to dance!

When will you dance?

_____
_____
_____
_____
_____
_____
_____
_____
_____
_____
_____
_____
_____
_____
_____

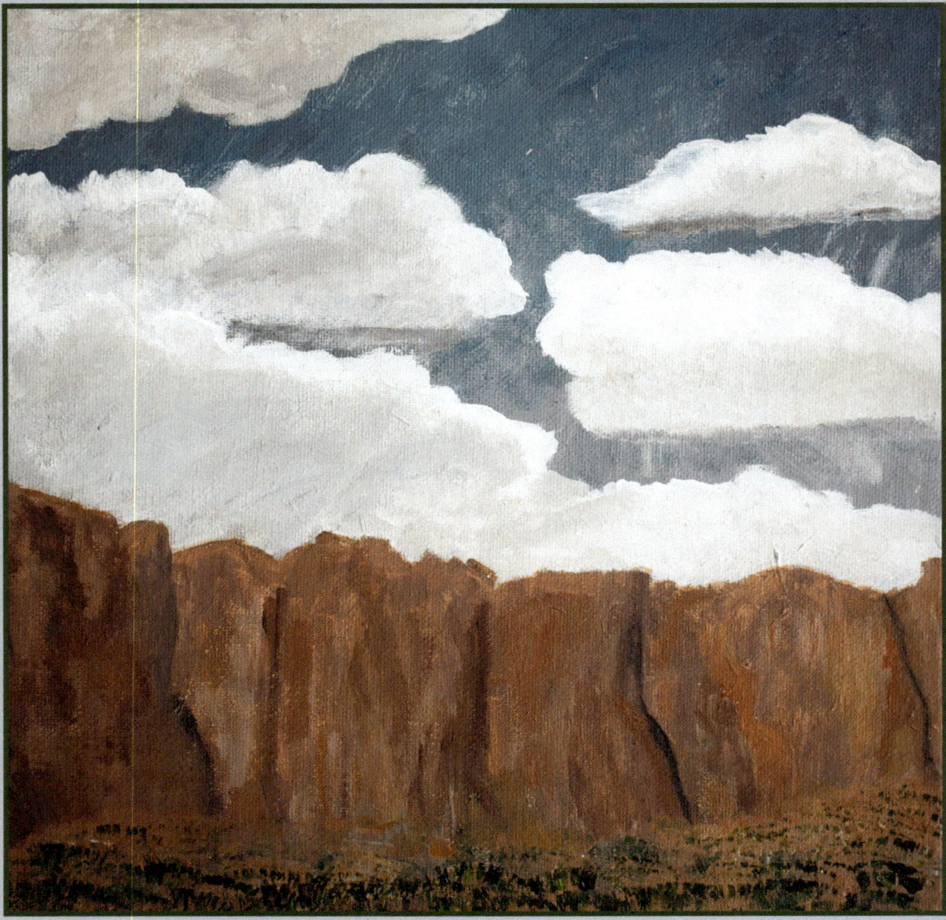

Monsoon Moments

In a monsoon moment,
heat cedes the fight
and shadows crawl
from under rocks,
creeping across
the desert floor.

Silhouettes of clouded light
amass to shade the earth

In silent song

And the air releases
a sweet scent of creosote
while delicate drops of rain
slip through the air
to cling to Palo Verde spines
before they

float

to tap the earth.

Anon, a shaft of light,
an aberration in the sky
like a soprano's voice in sudden
aria—pure beauty, extraordinary
phenomenon, ignites
a glimpse at heaven's flame

The precursor of percussion

Powerful baritone booms
jarring all to listen
to a crescendo of thunder
and rain, a precious downpour
that sings momentary

harmony.

Earth glistening

Before a gentle pianissimo concludes
the monsoon symphony of life.

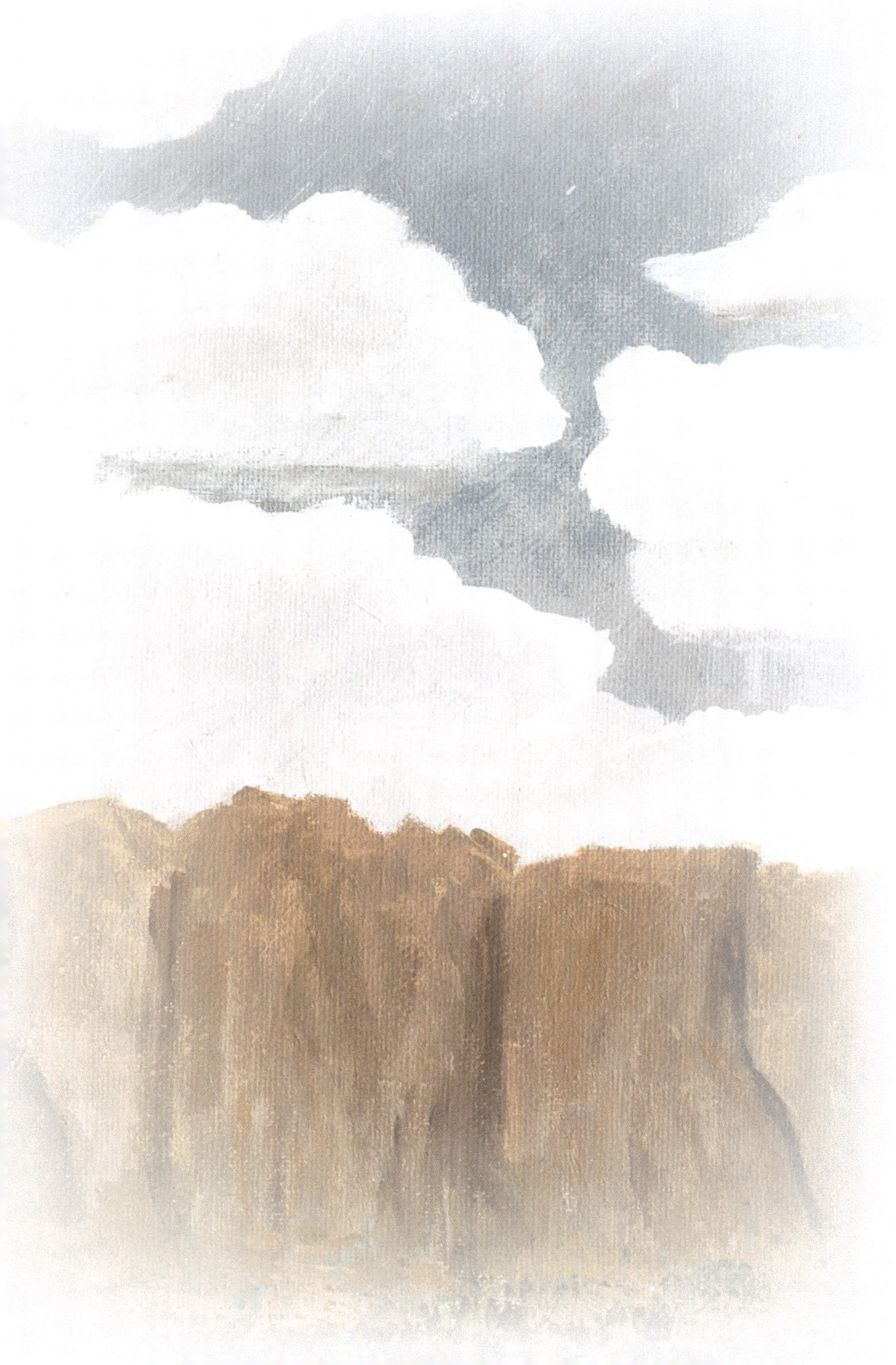

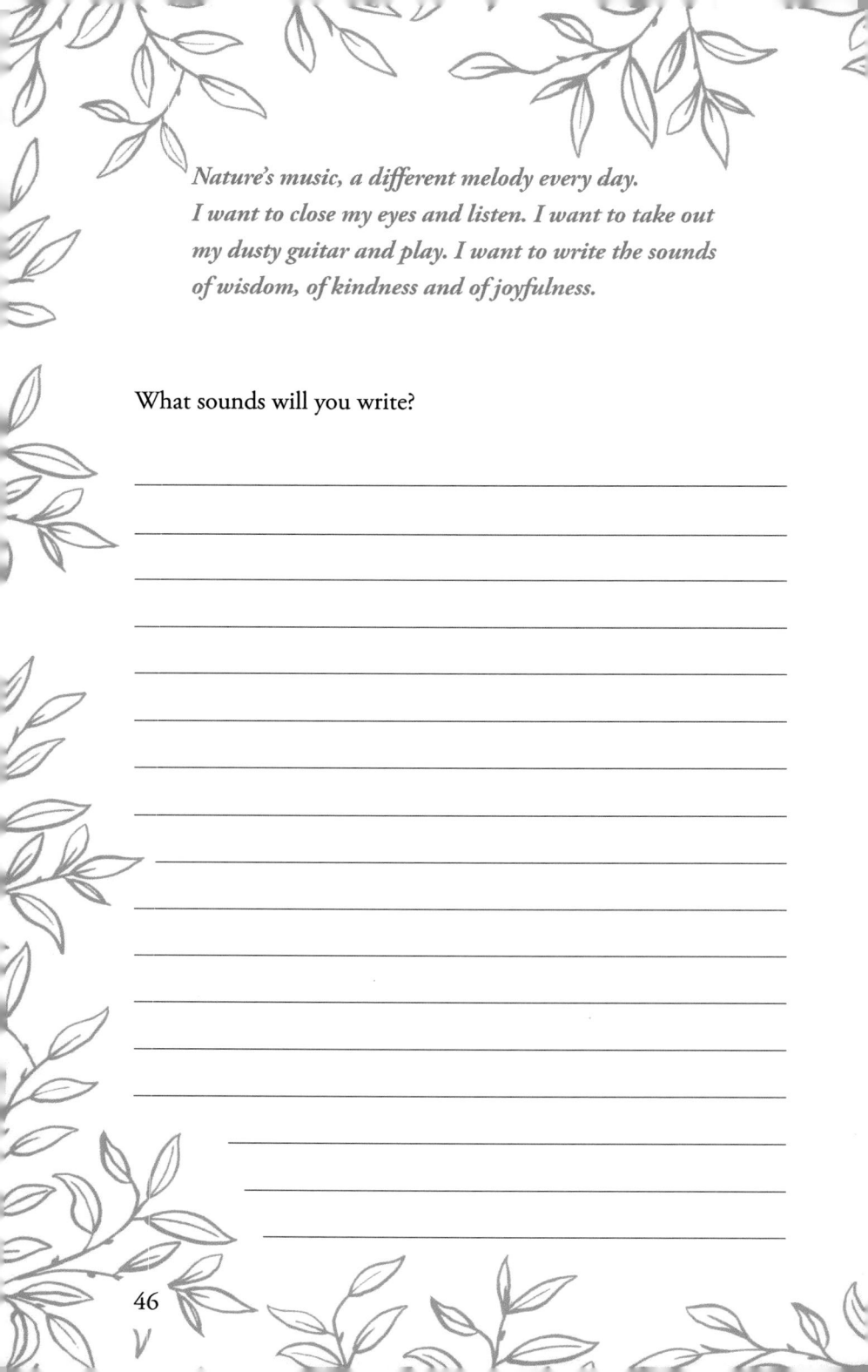

Nature's music, a different melody every day. I want to close my eyes and listen. I want to take out my dusty guitar and play. I want to write the sounds of wisdom, of kindness and of joyfulness.

What sounds will you write?

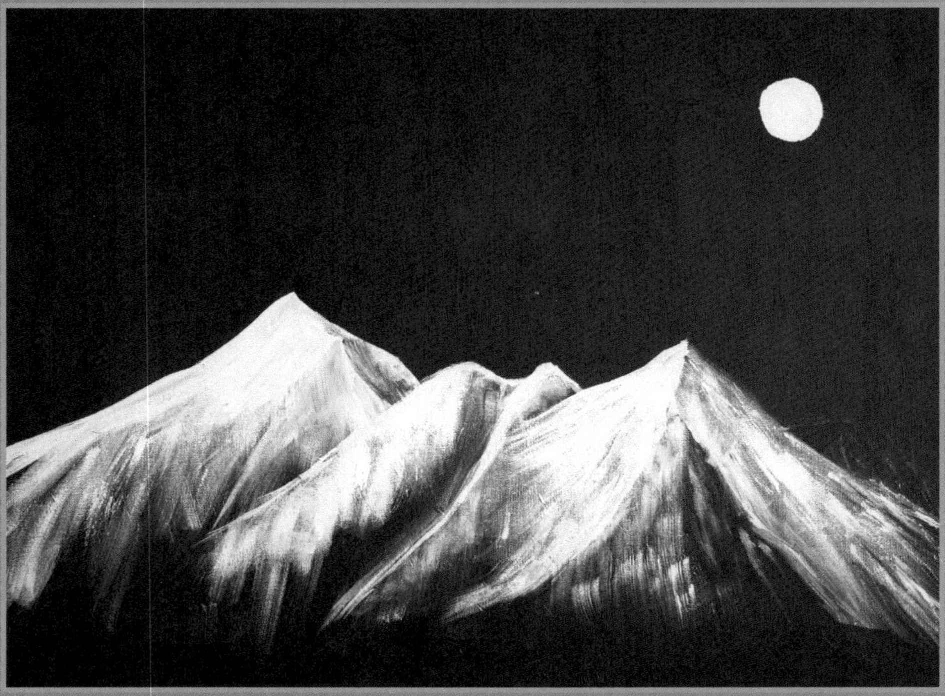

Love Above the Trees

Amid the mountains
Lie the secrets of
Eternal love.
Foothills softly slope

Ascending into powerful
Peaks above.

Only souls fit for the
Long hike
Committed to the trek
Willing to breathe
Thin air
Survive

To see the pure white snow
To touch its icy wonder
To know the power
Of being alive.

Loving another
Forever

Requires strength
of a similar kind,
Like the earth's
Toughest climbs,

Love tests the
Spirit and the
Mind

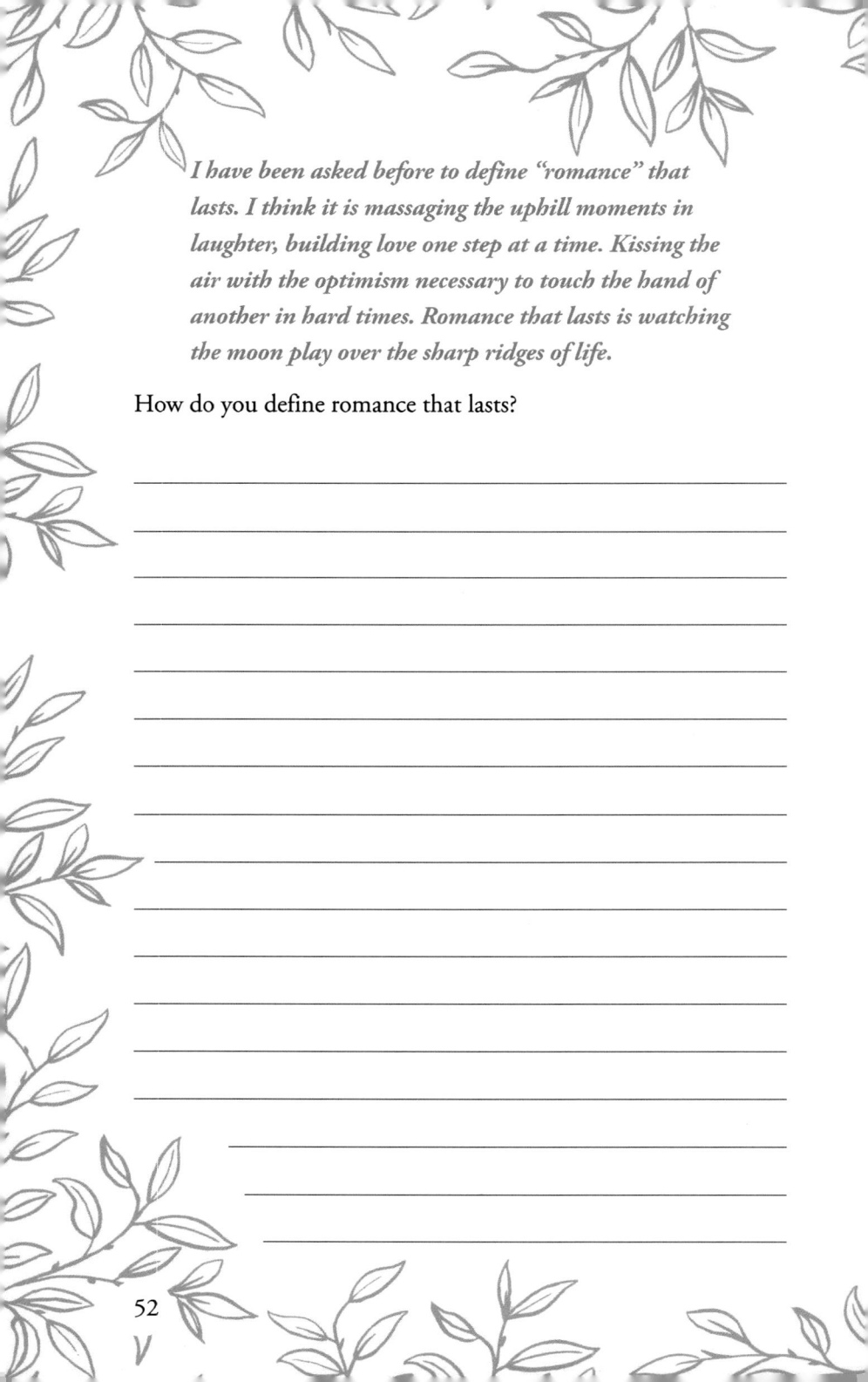

I have been asked before to define "romance" that lasts. I think it is massaging the uphill moments in laughter, building love one step at a time. Kissing the air with the optimism necessary to touch the hand of another in hard times. Romance that lasts is watching the moon play over the sharp ridges of life.

How do you define romance that lasts?

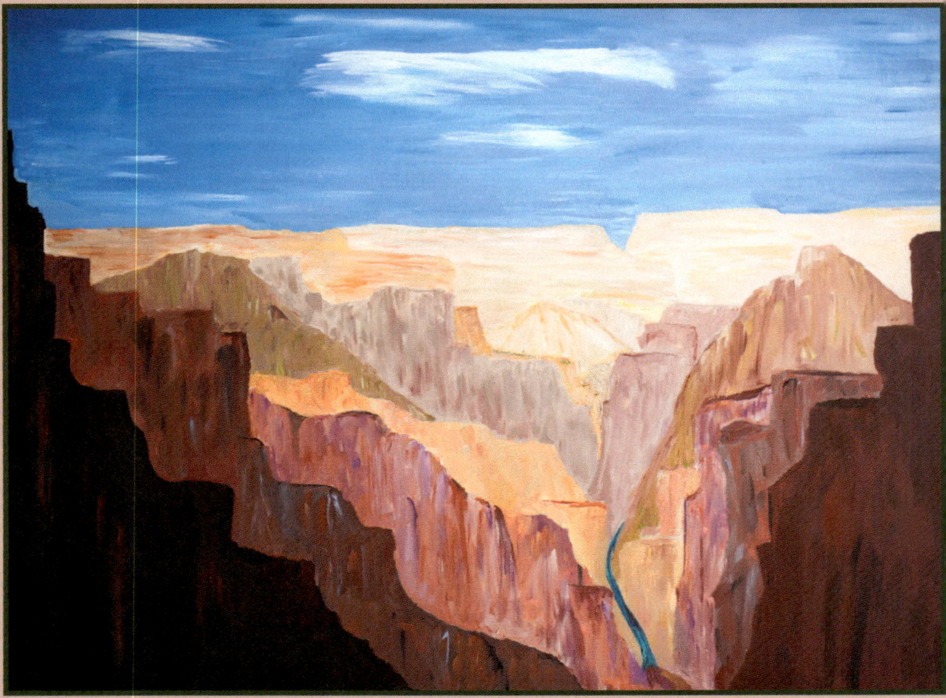

Spirit Gift

Spirit gift

Peaceful lift

Water, life

Flowing through

Eons, ages

Sculpted time

Descends, ascends

The moment wends.

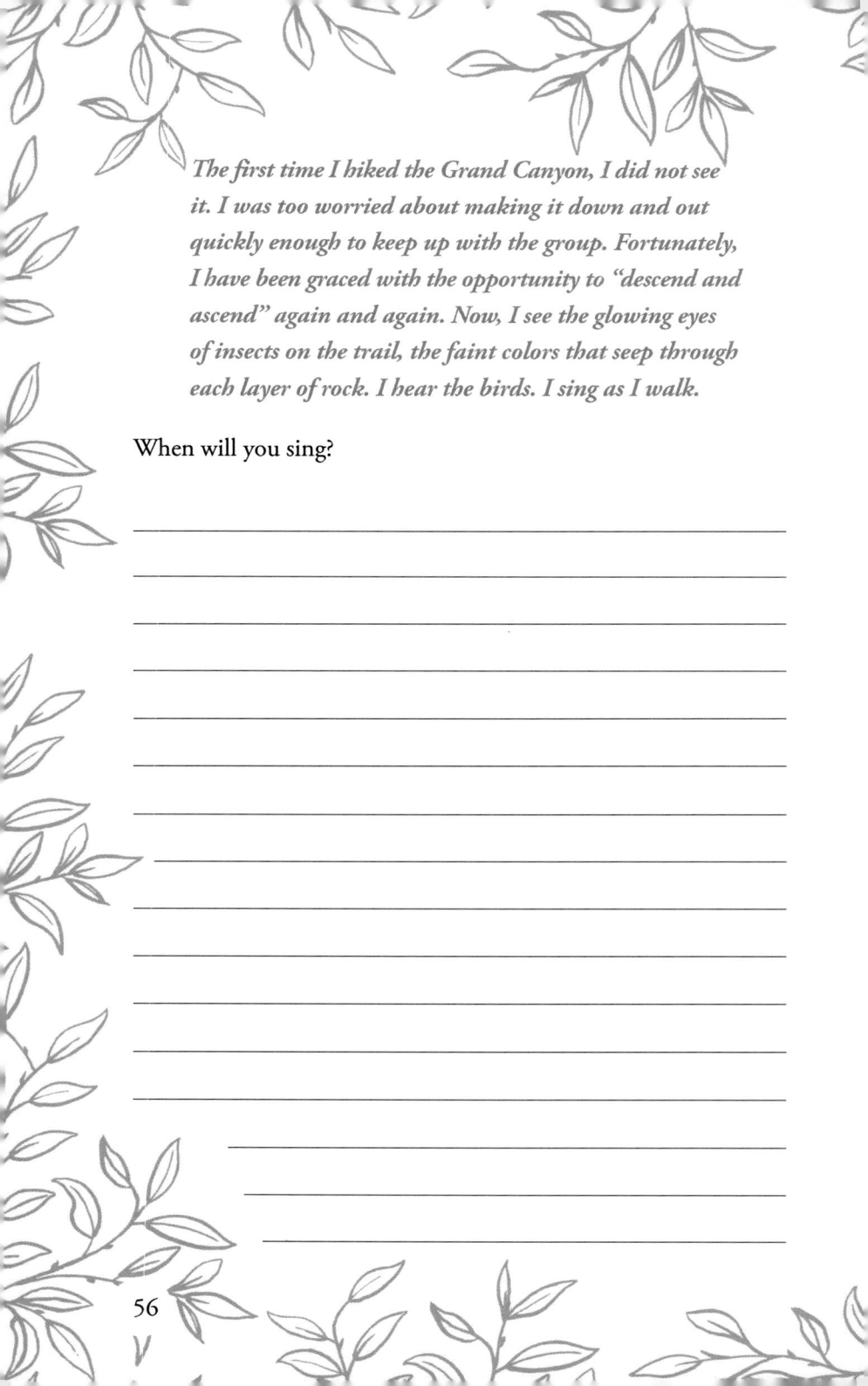

The first time I hiked the Grand Canyon, I did not see it. I was too worried about making it down and out quickly enough to keep up with the group. Fortunately, I have been graced with the opportunity to "descend and ascend" again and again. Now, I see the glowing eyes of insects on the trail, the faint colors that seep through each layer of rock. I hear the birds. I sing as I walk.

When will you sing?

_____
_____
_____
_____
_____
_____
_____
_____
_____
_____
_____
_____
_____
_____

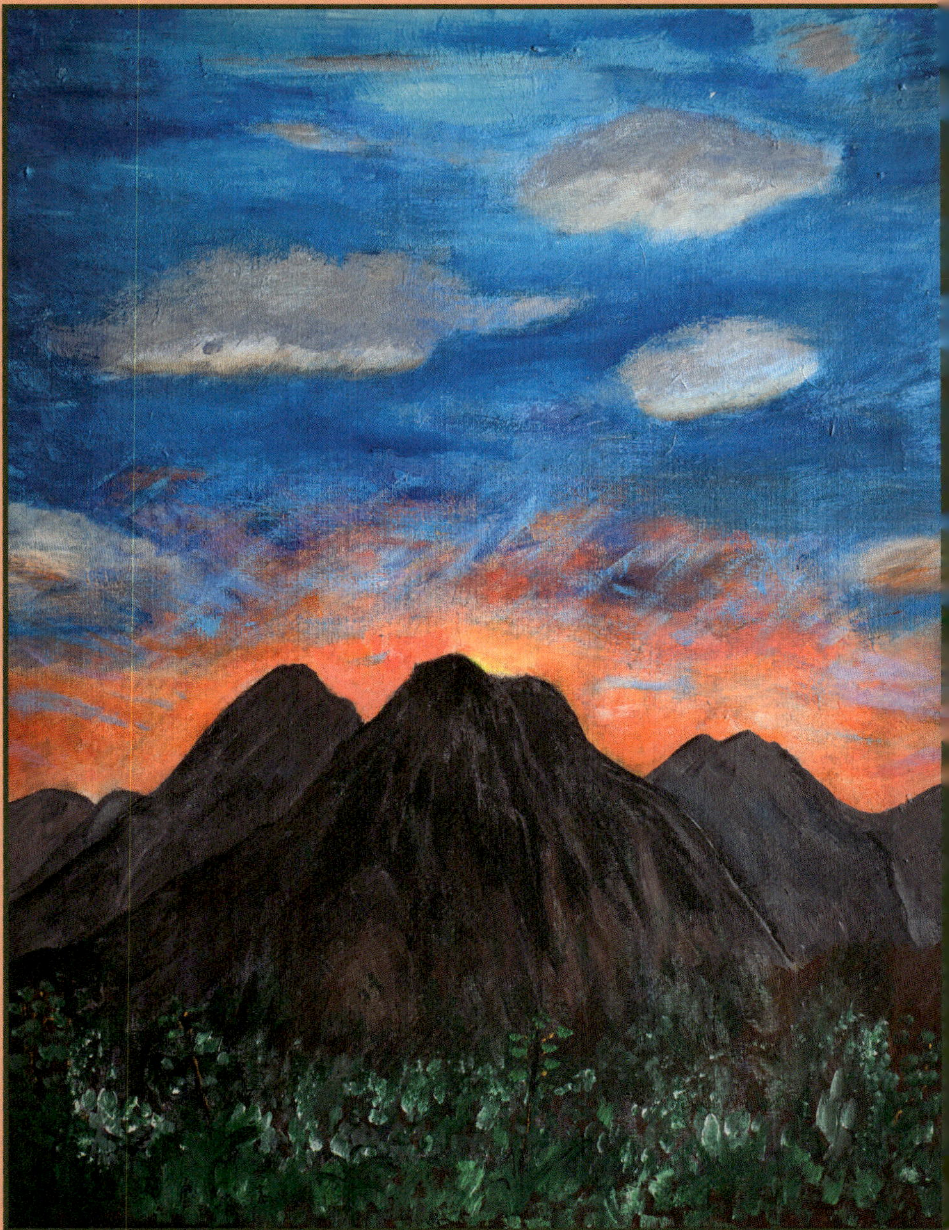

When Words Falter

Sometimes silence
Scripts

When words
Falter,

West aflame

In an instant

Radiant fingers
Touch heaven

I am a purveyor of words. Sometimes minding my moments necessitates quietude. I am learning to silence my thoughts and let the moment move through me. Much of what "touches heaven" isn't bound in language.

How do you acknowledge your need for silence? Before you write, spend a few minutes clearing your head of language. When you come back, just write your first thoughts.

_____
_____
_____
_____
_____
_____
_____
_____
_____
_____
_____
_____

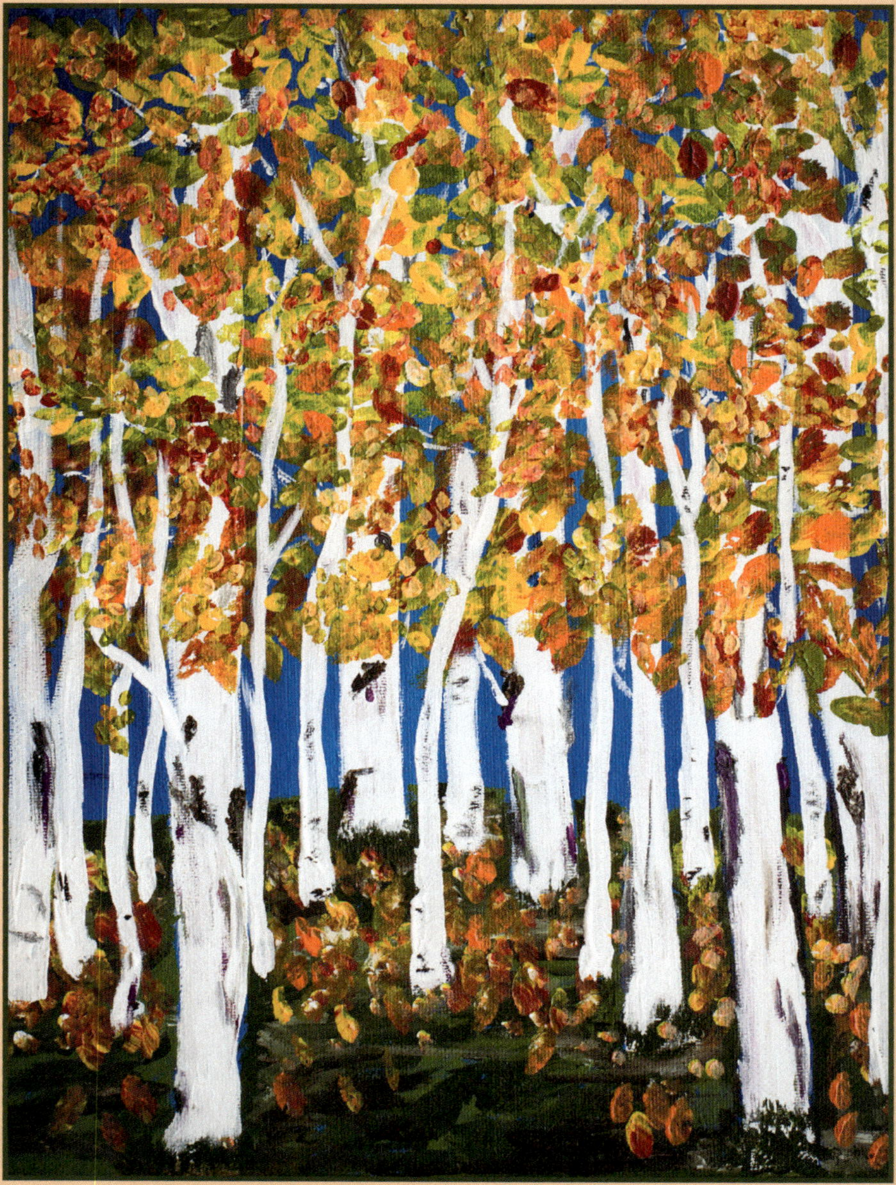

Wind

The wind alone is voiceless,
It must have a mate
Only coupled with the trees,
Can a message, wind create.

Listen to the leaves
As with the wind
They whisper
And they quake.

Together they romance
The air
And ticklish
Laughter make.

Alone time is important to me, but I have realized that sharing my moments is part of minding them. Human interaction, friends, lovers, families are great gifts. I have "lost touch" with important people in my life. Taking the time to "ticklish laughter make," to write a letter, pick up the phone, send an email, was time I didn't find. I cherish those who have always found the time to stay connected with me. I now set "connecting" as a priority, and the time is suddenly there. Sharing moments, even briefly, make me more alive.

How do you keep connected? Who is someone you have lost? What moment would you like to share with him/her? Write it here with a plan to make the moment happen. When you have, come back and write the "ticklish laughter" made.

_____
_____
_____
_____
_____
_____
_____
_____

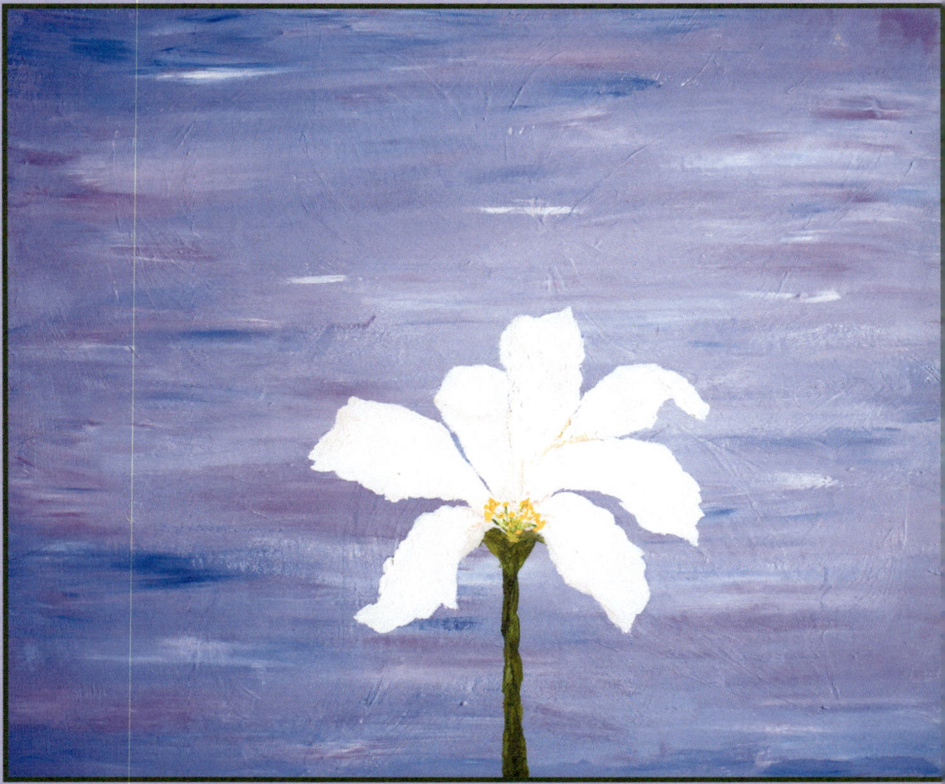

Evening Flower

Wrinkled from the sun
left to stand strong

alone

in the purple gauze
that shimmers when the earth

pivots

away from the light
into the dusk's

iridescence.

In soliloquy, she
proclaims artistic

antiquity

reigning the evening
in brilliant

 harmony

Radiantly illuminating
her space

quaint

petals white as
the moon,

blushing

in the afterglow
of her day's long

Life.

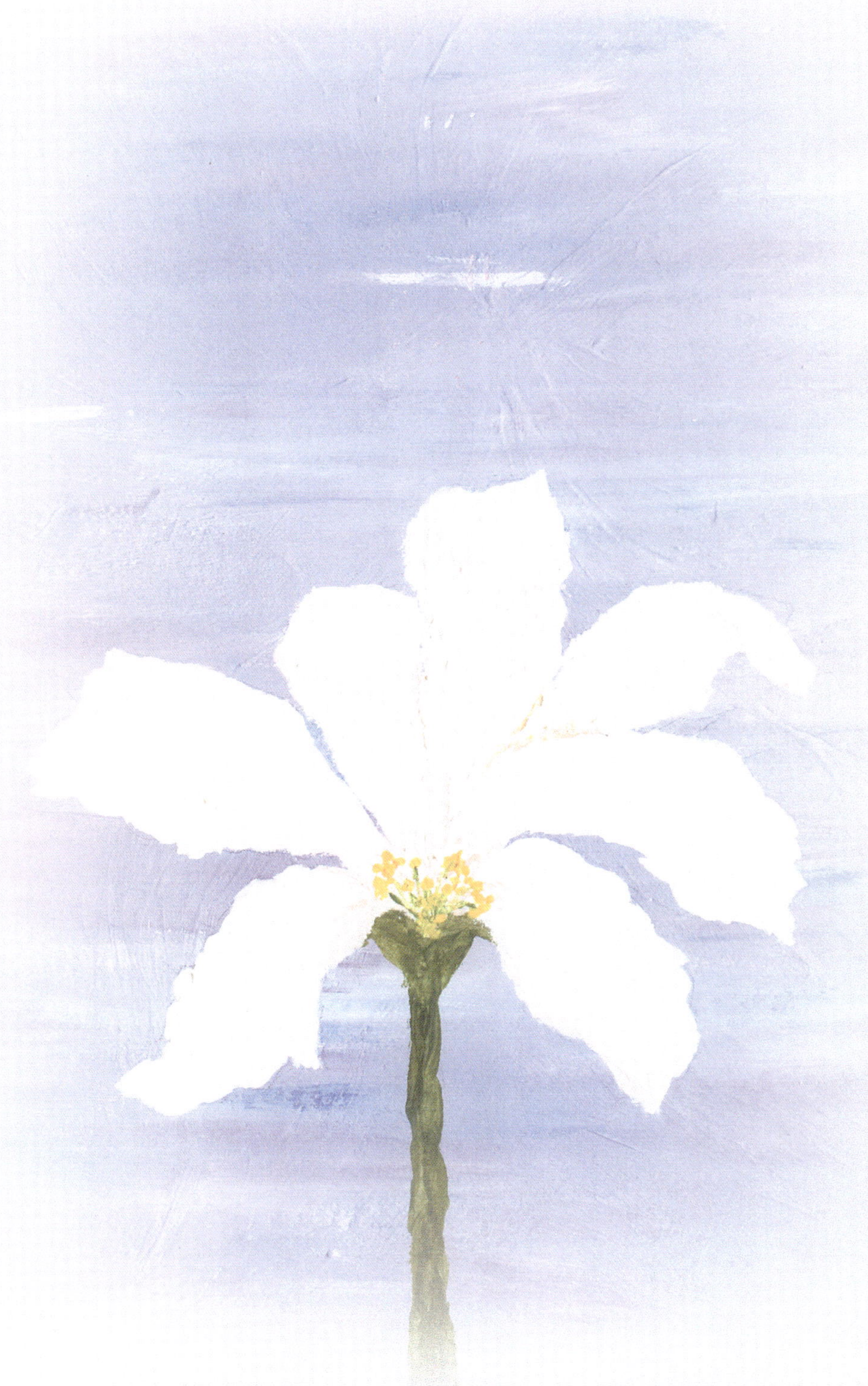

Many words describe us when we accumulate a myriad of moments, "old, aged, elderly." But I have had the opportunity to share some special time with "evening flowers" who radiate strength and beauty. They appreciate every moment past and present. In the last moments I spent with my grandfather, we sang. We sang so loudly, the hospital nurse told us to "keep it down." We kept singing. I love the memory of that moment. In my heart, I will always sing with him.

What special moment have you shared with an "evening flower?" Or, who is an "evening flower" in your life, and how will you share a special moment?

_____
_____
_____
_____
_____
_____
_____
_____
_____
_____

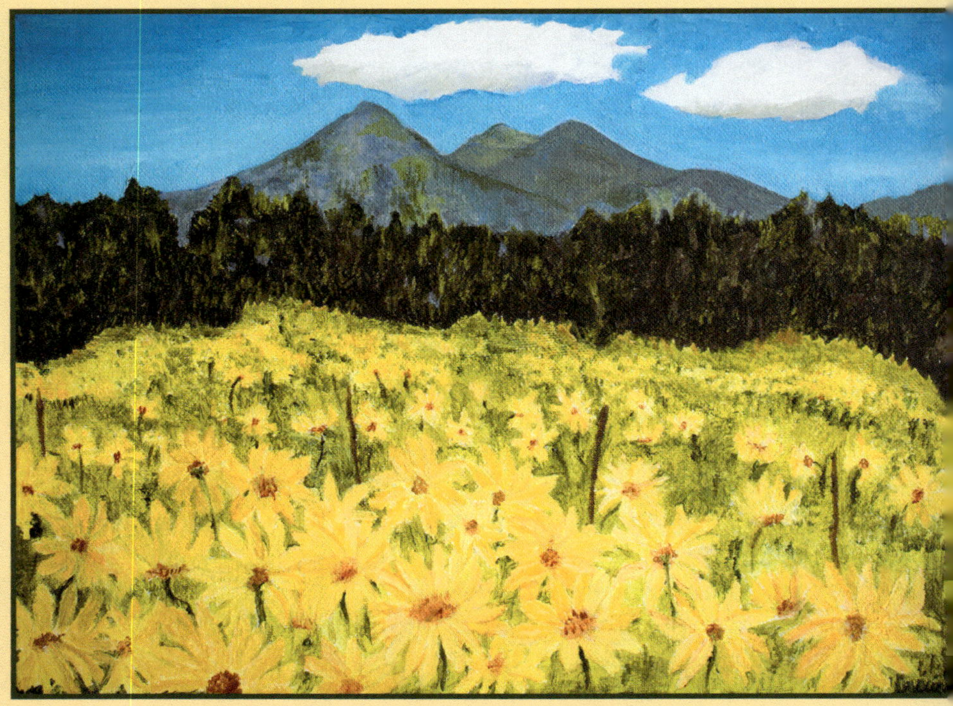

A Moment's Perspective

My gaze
Falls upon a yellow field
And sends my mind
To love revealed.

Her eyes lock upon
Movement in the trees
She imagines a quiet
Moment in the breeze.

He sees nothing
But the sacred peaks
His mind floats
To the heights he seeks.

They look up and find
Shapes among the clouds
Fantasies a child's perspective
Is allowed.

The scene is shaped in
The instant of a thought
Each a worthy whisper
Of what the others sought.

I believe minding my own moments, allows me to be more empathetic with the perspectives of others. When I seek clarity of my own thoughts, I gain the peace of mind it takes to seek to understand how others mind their moments. I also broaden my ability to appreciate my own moments opening my mind to a bigger picture.

Reflect on a time when you saw a "moment" very differently from someone else. How did you respond? Was each perspective warranted? What does it help you learn about how you consider your own moments?

_____

_____

_____

_____

_____

_____

_____

_____

_____

_____

_____

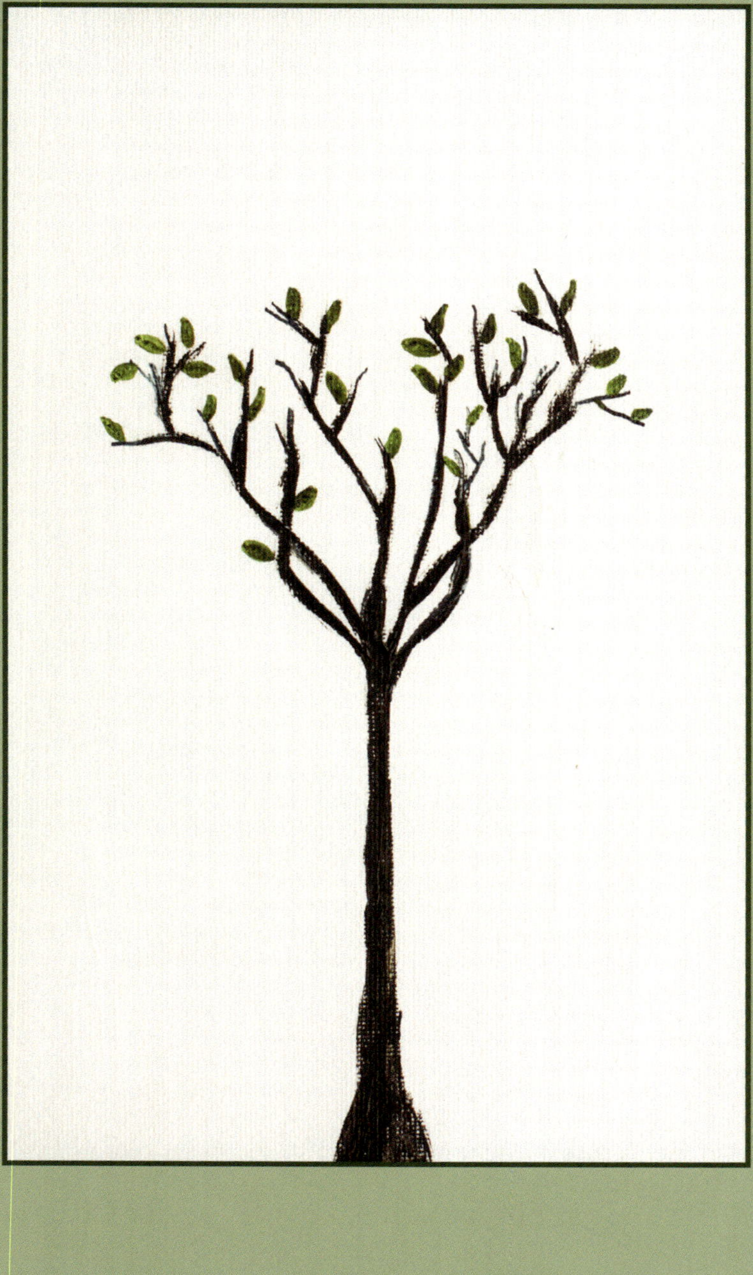

Growing in the Moment

Even the simplest
tree
Reaches up,

Every inch
A feat,

Every leaf
A reason to go on.

Even the simplest
Tree
Feels the morning
Warmth
And lifts its
limbs
Upward, outward
. . . Seeking.

Even the simplest tree
Explores a greater
Space.

Even the simplest
Tree
Finds strength
From its moments

In the sun.

I love to learn, but I often want to absorb new knowledge quickly, to "get it" on my first try. I am learning to be like the "simplest tree" to appreciate the moments of struggle as much as I appreciate the moments of victory. I need to learn to mind my moments of failure and grow from them. When "rush" overcomes me, I feel defeated; I want to give up. When enjoying my "moments in the sun" and absorbing the warmth slowly, finding growth in tiny leaves, I feel progress. Tranquility enfolds me and allows me to move on. My new mantra is "even the simplest tree" which reminds me to lift my spirits, accept myself and my own "reason to go on."

How do you learn? What keeps you going in the face of defeat? Write about a moment when you wanted to give up, but chose to grow. What is a mantra you could use to keep you finding strength in your "moments in the sun."

_____
_____
_____
_____
_____
_____
_____
_____
_____

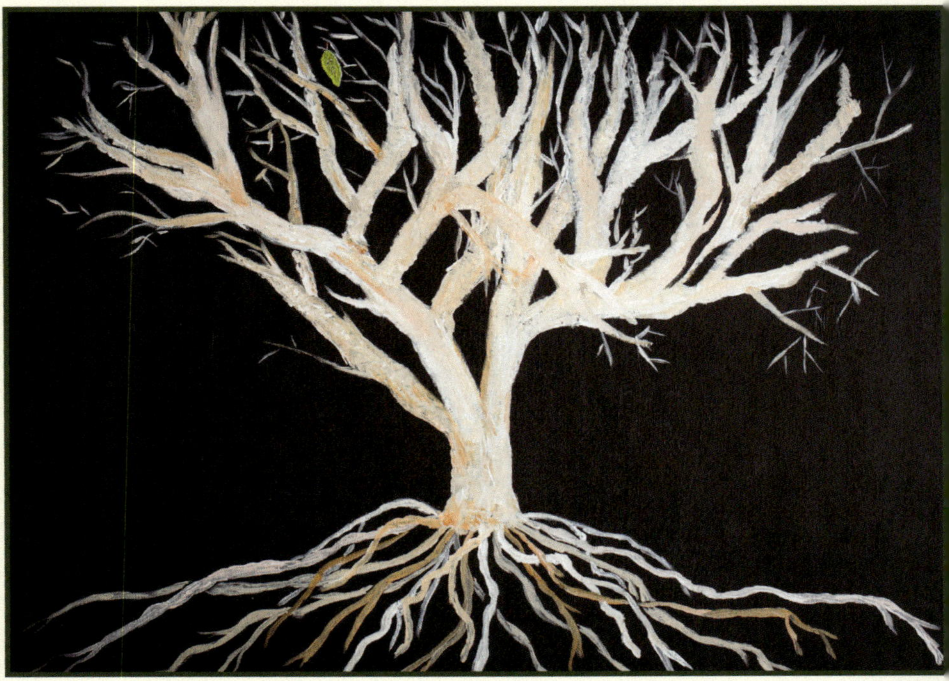

Tree of Hope

Dark, light
Etchings hued
With age

Reaching up,
Plunging downward
Splintered time

Inhale, exhale
Solitary
Sign of life

Looming, delicate
Mercy,
Sunlight,
Moisture

Green,
Rebirth,
Future,
Hope

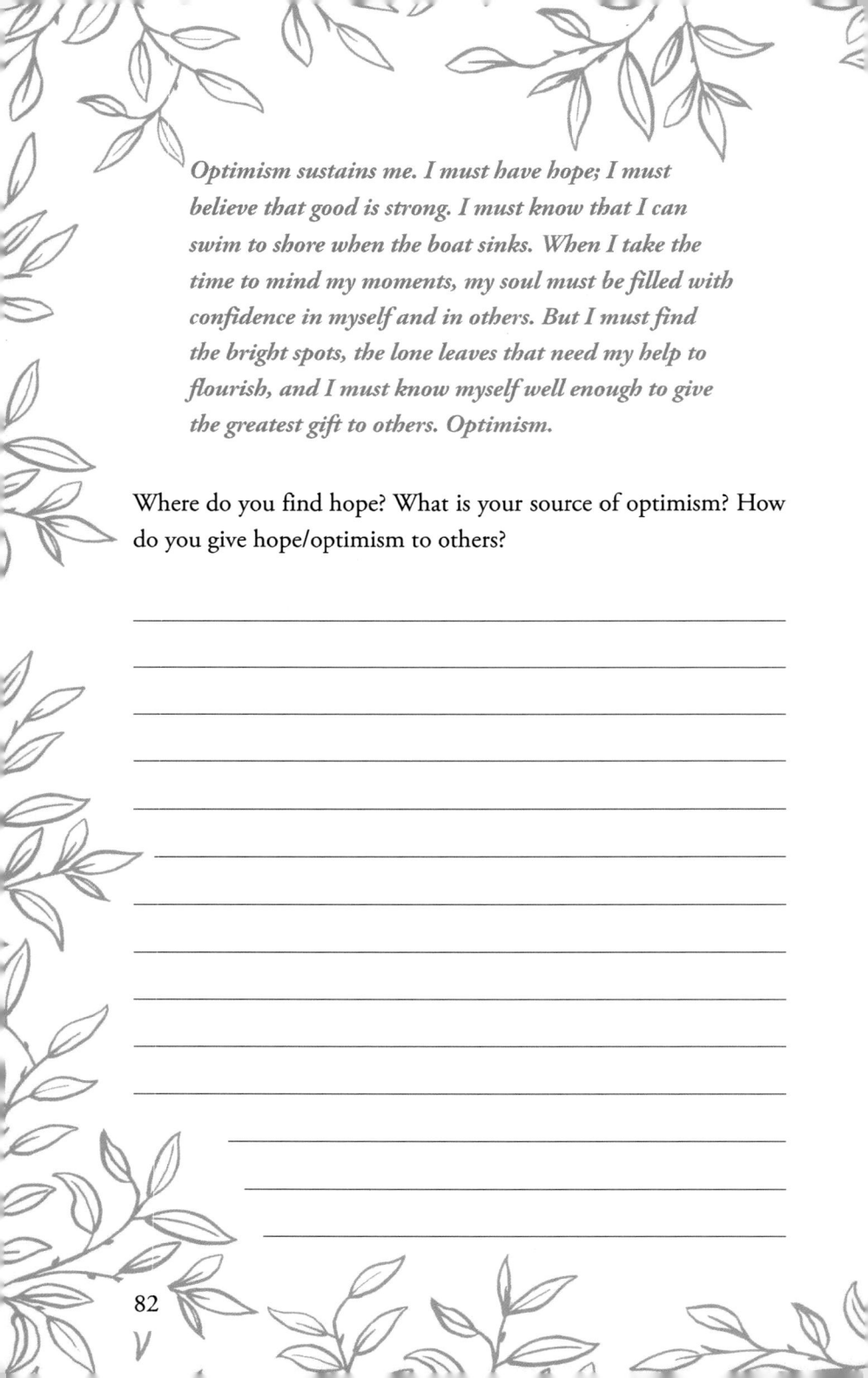

Optimism sustains me. I must have hope; I must believe that good is strong. I must know that I can swim to shore when the boat sinks. When I take the time to mind my moments, my soul must be filled with confidence in myself and in others. But I must find the bright spots, the lone leaves that need my help to flourish, and I must know myself well enough to give the greatest gift to others. Optimism.

Where do you find hope? What is your source of optimism? How do you give hope/optimism to others?

_____
_____
_____
_____
_____
_____
_____
_____
_____
_____
_____

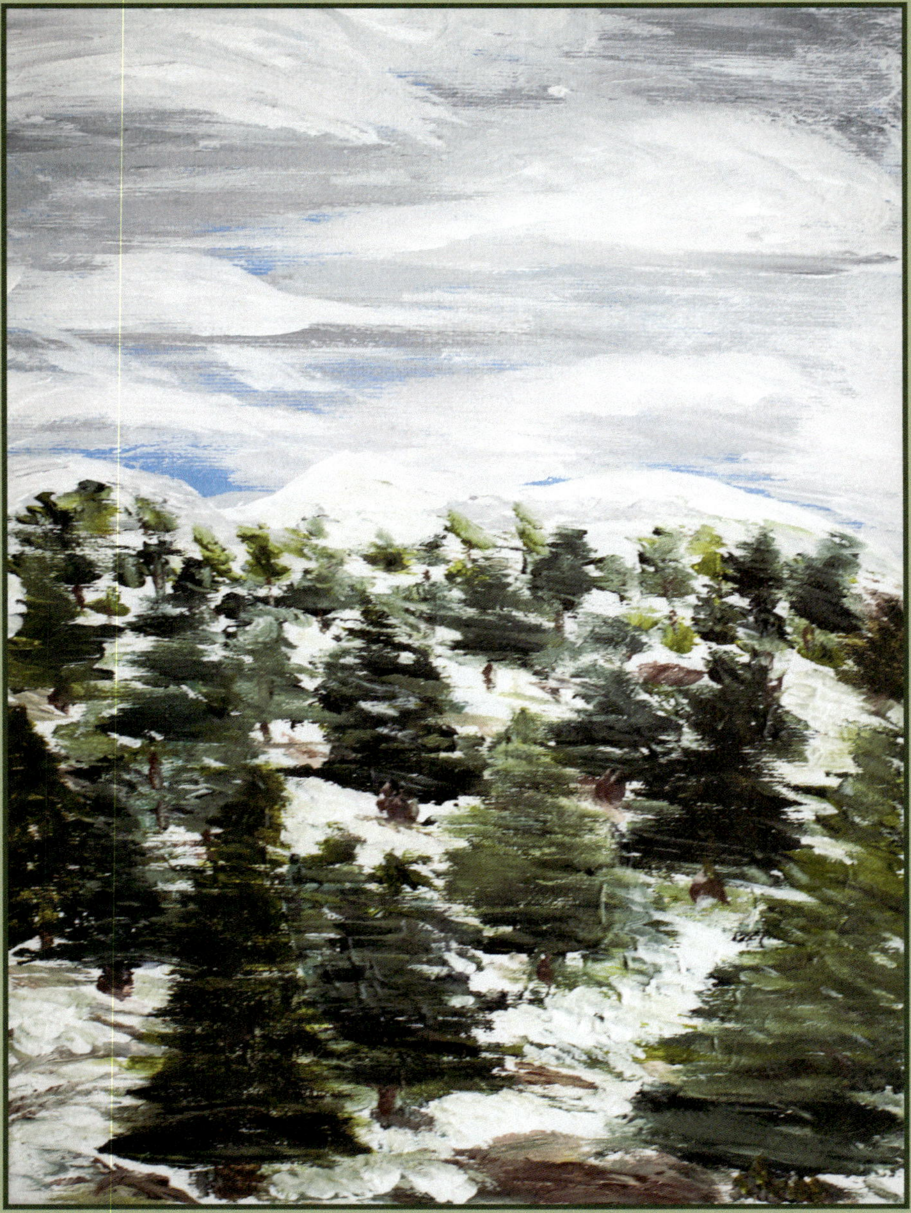

Blurred Moments

Sometimes I cannot see
Where one moment ends
And sets the next one free

Like trees in a frosted wood,
Edges disappear
Softened in a clouded hood

My eyes let me believe
That it is mine to define
Where lines interweave

Mine to decide
The virtue of the view
Clarity cast aside

The haze is the allure
To the tenderness of
A mountainside of blur

I am comfortable in chaos. I have learned many others are not. I do find tenderness in not having to define all the lines of life. I like spontaneity; I struggle making plans. However, the blur sometimes encourages me to let life happen to me instead of seeing the path that makes the most sense. Sometimes that means I spend time lost. So I allow myself some time on the blurry mountainside; where pathways are vague, and I can wend my way around the trees. But I have learned that putting that creative thought in focus can help me relate to those who find the blur distracting. I mix poetry with prose and hope my message makes meaning to many.

Do you love the blur or care for someone who does? How do you make meaning? Are you poetry or prose? Which moments move you forward?

_____

_____

_____

_____

_____

_____

_____

_____

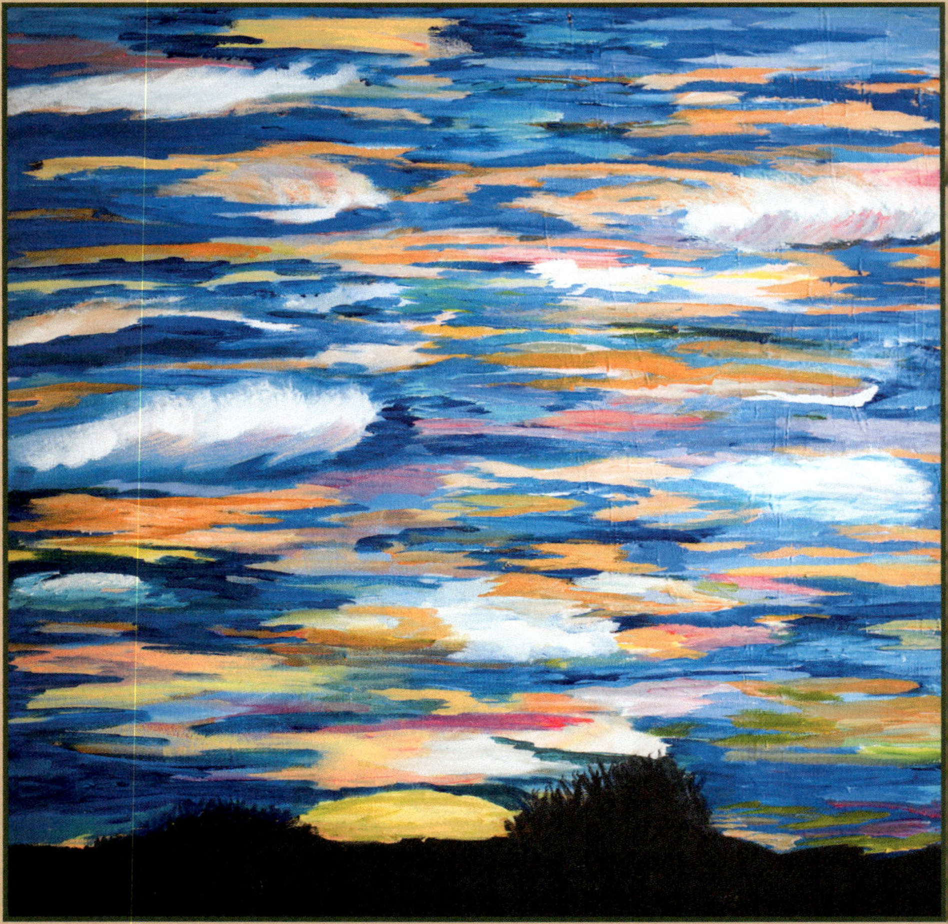

Playful Moments

No lines
To stay inside

All the colors
In the box

Spill their hues
And collide

Upon the canvas.

Unconstrained
Like a thought

Finding a
Creative muse

A silly moment
Sought

At end of day

My last mind your moment reminder, everyone needs some time just to be silly. I let my mind wander, listen to my muse and find myself with a ridiculous grin—and people staring. Let them stare. I am outside the lines for a moment. I will be back, soon enough.

When do you color outside the lines? What is your silly thought?

_____
_____
_____
_____
_____
_____
_____
_____
_____
_____
_____
_____

PREVIEW OF

*Into the
Hand I Hold*

MIND YOUR MOMENTS SERIES • BOOK TWO

Into the Hand I Hold

Her strength
runs through me,
Straightens my stance
squares my shoulders.
Often I can feel her,
seeing with my eyes
Clearing my vision
—rather than the path.
In the mirror I watch
her unwavering countenance
But when I turn away,
I know the weakness
That must have been hers, too.

How could I have known
the hand with which
She so sturdily
pulled me through life
Was her balance?
—that my resistance
Held her upright and
built the muscle
Of her powerful influence
over those she touched
Her strength
runs through me
Into the hand I hold.